ALL THINGS PROCEED

A REGNUM CHRISTI ESSAY ON RECOGNITION AND COMMUNION

FR. JOHN PIETROPAOLI, LC, STL

ISBN-10: 1534921834

ISBN-13: 9781534921832

RC Essay Editorial Review Board:

Fr. John Bartunek, LC, SThD
Fr. Daniel Brandenburg, LC, PhL, SThL
Lucy Honner, CRC
Rebecca Teti, CatholicDigest.com writer and editor

TABLE OF CONTENTS

FOREWORD

FOREWORD: WHAT ARE RC ESSAYS?

RC Essays are extended, in-depth reflections on particular aspects of life as a Regnum Christi member. An Essay may develop the nature of a virtue, showing what that virtue might look like when lived out in harmony with the Regnum Christi identity and mission. An Essay may explore the challenges of living out one of the commitments shared by all members. An Essay may be instructive, explaining the history, context, and meaning of certain Movement traditions. In short, RC Essays are a chance for all of us to delve deeper into our charism, reflecting seriously on our spiritual patrimony, which the Church has recognized and lauded, and in that way helping that patrimony grow and bear fruit.

RC Essays make no pretense of being the sole and exhaustive expression of our charism. The RC Spirituality Center will review and edit them to ensure their quality in expression and content, but no single person owns a collective charism in such a way as to give it a definitive and exhaustive expression. This is one of the important lessons we have begun to learn in our process of reform and renewal.

Some RC Essays will lend themselves naturally to personal meditation; others will be especially apt for group study circles; all aim to be useful as spiritual reading for members in every branch of the Movement.

It is our hope and prayer that this series will continue to grow organically under the Holy Spirit's guidance. Some Essays will connect more strongly with our members, and others less, while some may fall by the wayside after their useful moment has passed. Yet perhaps the best

RC Essays will stand the test of time, becoming spiritual and intellectual nourishment for many generations of Movement members.

Please send your ideas and feedback to us through the feedback button at RCSpirituality.org.

ALL THINGS
PROCEED

INTRODUCTION

❝Love is the human person's essential vocation.

—*Regnum Christi Member Handbook*, Number 3

❝In the heart of the Church, my Mother, I will be Love.

—St. Therese of Lisieux, *Story of a Soul*

In his spiritual diary, Thomas Merton recorded the following experience:

❝In Louisville, at the corner of Fourth and Walnut, in the center of the shopping district, I was suddenly overwhelmed with the realization that I loved all those people, that they were mine and I theirs, that we could not be alien to one another even though we were total stranger ... I have the immense joy of being human, a member of a race in which God Himself became incarnate ... Then it was as if I suddenly saw the secret beauty of their hearts, the depths of their hearts ... the person that each one is in God's eyes. If only they could all see themselves as they really are. If only we could see each other that way all the time.

The term that comes to mind is "communion." The word itself is polysemous, but there seems to be a core meaning to it that makes our hearts leap when we hear it. It contains a promise that we can see another person—every other person—with new eyes because we see with a new heart.

We can glance at Michelangelo's *Pieta* a thousand times, yet when we peer into the depths it's as though we discover the statue for the first time. We can peruse W.B. Yeats or Dylan Thomas or T.S. Eliot, yet when we're finally struck by the drama of *Easter, 1916*, or the pathos of *A Poem in October*, or the lyrical mysticism of the *4 Quartets*, something shifts in our hearts. We can look into a human face and see nothing, or we can glimpse all the mystery and wonder and depth and sheer delight of the Blessed Trinity, that Communion of Persons whose love is inscribed into our very being. We are, perhaps, in exile, but we are not in isolation.

The term communion has considerable currency both in the Church and in Regnum Christi's renewal. We have a shared sense that God wants us to experience the gift of communion. But the term has a meaning far deeper than simply all getting along or treating each other in a civil fashion to get things done.

The new movements in the Church help give flesh and blood to the Universal Call to Holiness. And holiness, union with God, is only in communion. As John Zizioulas puts it in *Communion and Otherness*, "When the Holy Spirit breathes He does not create good individual Christians, individual saints, but an event of communion which transforms everything the Spirit touches into a relational being." We're called to transcend the labels of secularism/clericalism, right/left, conservative/liberal, and offer God's vision of the human person, whose richness lies not in contrast but in complementarity. Living and evangelizing in true communion—as lay people, consecrated men and women, and priests—we show that, with God, this is possible. And since what we pray and think about shapes our actions, further reflection on communion is both relevant and enriching. In T.S. Eliot's *Murder in the Cathedral*, Saint Thomas Becket declares: "I have had a tremor of bliss, a wink of heaven, a whisper, and I would no longer be denied. All things proceed to a joyful consummation." The experience of true communion is that glimpse of heaven that we can offer to an achingly anonymous world, and it's what we'll explore in the following essay.

WE ARE CHRIST'S

To understand Regnum Christi's mission you must begin with a need deeply rooted in the heart of each individual—the need for a personal encounter with Christ and his merciful and life-giving love.

—*Regnum Christi Member Handbook*, Number 28

The Person is otherness in communion, and communion in otherness ... an identity that emerges through relationship. It is an "I" that can exist only as long as it relates to a "Thou" which affirms its existence and its otherness.

—John Zizioulas, *Communion and Otherness*

We need to know that we belong, and that we matter to someone simply because we exist. I remember reading about a seamstress in a maximum security prison in New York who helped orchestrate an elaborate prison break for two convicted murderers. When asked why she did it, she replied that one of the convicts made her "feel special." We're naturally aghast at her actions, but doesn't her comment strike at the heart of things? Doesn't each

3

one of us need to know that we matter to someone? God certainly seems to think so.

In that regard, 587 B.C. was a singularly inauspicious year for God's chosen people. The Babylonians under Nebuchadnezzar sacked Jerusalem and destroyed the temple. The Holy of Holies, which held the Ark of the Covenant, was profaned and the Shekinah (the Divine Presence) seemed lost. To add insult to injury, the Babylonians forced the majority of Jerusalem's inhabitants into exile in Babylon, where they endured a servile existence for the next 50 or so years.

In the midst of this Babylonian captivity, God inspired Deutero-Isaiah, sometimes called "The Book of the Consolation of Israel." Isaiah 40–55 is God's reassurance to his people—and to each one of us—that we matter infinitely to him. His infinite care for us is movingly summed up in chapter 43, when the Lord says:

> Fear not, for I have redeemed you; I have called you by name, you are mine. When you pass through the waters I will be with you; and through the rivers, they will not overwhelm you … You are precious in my eyes, and glorious, and I love you.

Jesus makes this promise explicit in John 10:27–30 when he says:

> My sheep hear my voice, and I know them, and they follow me; and I give them eternal life, and they shall never perish, and no one shall snatch them out of my hand. My Father, who has given them to me, is greater than all, and no one is able to snatch them

out of the Father's hand. I and the Father are one.

Being a Christian means a living relationship with Jesus Christ. He has called us by name; we are his.

Our belonging to God creates a space for his love. Is communion legal, or is it existential? Is it an external structure, or does it flow from a new heart, a human heart touched and transformed by the Word made Flesh? In reality, it's both. Communion with the Lord, in the Church, is the foundation of all interpersonal communion. And just as Christ in the Eucharist (Communion in the most vivid sense imaginable) is the living heartbeat of the Church, our hearts united with his are the cause of any true structures of communion.

And because of this, we cannot conceive of life without communion among ourselves. St. Paul puts it like this in his letter to the Ephesians:

❝For he [Jesus] is our peace, who has made us both one, and has broken down the dividing wall of hostility by abolishing in his flesh the law of commandments and ordinances, that he might create in himself one new man in the place of two, so making peace, and might reconcile us both to God in one body through the cross, thereby bringing the hostility to an end.

This is something more than a simple association of people gathered together to get the job done. This touches upon the very meaning of human existence. In the following chapter we'll delve into what this something more could be. In the meantime, these questions may aid further reflection.

QUESTIONS FOR FURTHER REFLECTION

1. How would I explain "communion"?

2. What experiences of belonging to God have touched me most deeply?

3. What experience of communion with others resonates most deeply in my heart?

4. Saint John Paul II said that the person who needs me most is also the person I most need. How have I experienced this in my own life?

RECOGNITION AND COMMUNION

❝The human person lives to love God in his neighbor, and he loves his neighbor to live in God. Doing so, he is consistent with his human nature, which bears the image and likeness of God.

—*Regnum Christi Member Handbook*, Number 4.

❝Dark and cold we may be, but this
Is no winter now. The frozen misery
Of centuries breaks, cracks, begins to move …
Thank God our time is now when wrong
Comes up to face us everywhere,
Never to leave us till we take
The longest stride of soul we ever took.
Affairs are now soul size.
The enterprise is exploration into God.

—Christopher Fry, "A Sleep of Prisoners"

AN INITIAL IDEA

Now the question arises, what is communion? To some extent that's like asking the question, what is life? You can attempt a technical definition, but the reality will always surpass our poor power to add or detract.

And yet there is one reality that takes up the question of communion and answers it as only God could. In the Eucharist we have that Communion upon which any experience of communion is founded, confirmed, and fully expressed.

This is why St. John Paul II wrote in *Christifideles Laici* that the fundamental meaning of communion

❝Speaks of the union with God brought about by Jesus Christ, in the Holy Spirit … Baptism is the door and the foundation of communion in the Church. The Eucharist is the source and summit of the whole Christian life (cf. Lumen Gentium, 11). The Body of Christ in the Holy Eucharist sacramentalizes this communion … and actually brings about the intimate bonds of communion among all the faithful in the Body of Christ which is the Church.

What happens when we receive Jesus in the Eucharist? We are transformed into the Beloved. In Pope Benedict XVI's moving phrase there's an "alchemy of being" willed by God. Christ chooses to make a gift of himself to us: every time we receive the Eucharist, that gift is given again in complete freshness and newness.

The Eucharist is an experience of true life, a joyful encounter with God who is entirely Other, and yet also suddenly

Not-Other. Jesus united Himself to our humanity so that we "might have life, and have it abundantly" (John 10:10).

THE VISION OF GOD

In his tract "Against Heresies," Saint Irenaeus of Lyon made the famous statement "The glory of God is man fully alive." The second part of that phrase is less famous, but equally important: "And the life of man is the vision of God." What precisely does this mean? One interpretation is that our vision of God is our life (vis-à-vis the beatific vision), and this is true.

Another possible interpretation approaches the mystery of communion from a different angle. The life of man is God's vision of us. As we begin to experience how God looks at us, individually, with love, we begin to truly live. As God's glance of infinite love and delight touches our hearts, we begin to turn that same glance towards other people with a new recognition.

Cardinal Ratzinger brings this relationship into vivid focus in *Christianity and the Crisis of Cultures*:

The decision for good or evil begins with our eyes, when we choose whether or not to look at the face of the other...The other is the custodian of my own dignity ... But we can only succeed in looking at others in a manner that respects their personal dignity if we experience how God looks at us in love ... The drama of our times consists precisely in our incapacity to look at ourselves as God does—and that is why we find it threatening to look at the other and must protect ourselves against it.

When we allow ourselves to be recognized by God we also begin to recognize others. We are known by God; in that being known we also know, and this knowing is life, this knowing is recognition, this knowing is, ultimately, communion.

TO KNOW IS TO LIVE

In English, the verb "to know" tends to be associated with a simple apprehension of fact. For example, I "know" that the boiling point of water is 212° Fahrenheit, or I "know" that the New York Yankees are the preeminent team in major league baseball history. However I might also say that I "know" a particular person as a casual acquaintance, and here we're clearly moving beyond the previous categorization and entering the realm of human relationships. The word is the same, but the meaning has suddenly become infinitely greater.

More significantly still, we say that we truly "know" someone when we can communicate with that person in a fully human way—and this means a sense of union, a recognition in my heart that this person is unique and precious and necessary. It's important to note that in Hebrew the verb to know—yada—has many layers of meaning, but in its primordial biblical usage it indicates a sense of intimacy, a glimpse of communion, and a promise of love and of life.

So when Jesus says in John 17:3 "In this is eternal life, that they know you the only true God and Jesus Christ whom you have sent," he's indicating something far more inspiring than a simple knowledge that God exists. He's promising a relationship that touches and transforms our hearts and our lives. Knowledge—recognition—is life, because it's a look of love. Communion is possible because of Christ who makes all things new, and who gives us back to God, to ourselves, and to each other.

This is life as God created it in the beginning; this is life restored to us in Christ.

UNION OF BEING

In his book *Jesus of Nazareth*, Pope Benedict XVI sums this up in one packed sentence: "Recognizing creates communion, which is union of being with the one recognized." This refers first and foremost true in our relationship with God. I am recognized by my Creator and Redeemer. In turn I recognize him, and this becomes communion, it becomes union of being with the One recognized. Participation in that communion, in that union of being with the one recognized which is the essence of the inner life of the Blessed Trinity, is offered to each one of us.

But there is more. Jesus asks the Father "That they may all be one; even as you, Father, are in me and I in You ..." (John 17:21). The communion with the Father, through the Son, in the Holy Spirit, which is offered to each one of us is meant to include others. In Jesus, there can be a new recognition of the other which becomes communion— union of being with the one recognized. Communion is identity recognized and expressed.

This union of being with the one recognized is, to my mind, the most compelling description of communion imaginable. But what does it look like? Perhaps some examples from Sacred Scripture can help.

The second chapter of the book of Genesis presents the primordial example. "Then the Lord God said, "It is not good that the man should be alone ..." God then proceeds to create a zoological cornucopia and the man names each animal. There is a real relationship—yet this relationship cannot express the fullness of that recognition and that communion which is the Blessed Trinity in whose image the man was created. The man recognizes something in each of the animals, but that recognition cannot be reciprocated. Although he can name them, none of the animals can name him.

So the Lord God caused a deep sleep to fall upon the man, and while he slept took one of his ribs and closed up its place with flesh; and the rib which the Lord God had taken from the man he made into a woman and brought her to the man. Then the man said, "This at last is bone of my bones and flesh of my flesh; she shall be called Woman, because she was taken out of Man."

The man's first recorded words are an expression of full recognition, of reverence and of wonder, of a union of being with the one recognized.

Saint John Paul II describes this encounter of the man and the woman in moving language.

In this way, in creating man as man and woman, God imprints on humanity the mystery of that communion which is the essence of his interior life. Man is drawn up into the mystery of God by the fact that his freedom is subjected to the law of love, and love creates interpersonal communion.

1 Samuel 18 furnishes another powerful instance of a union of being with the one recognized. David has just slain Goliath, and Saul asks to speak with him. Saul's son Jonathan is present and forges a friendship with David that the Bible describes in the following terms:

❝When [David] had finished speaking to Saul, the soul of Jonathan was knit to the soul of David, and Jonathan loved him as his own soul.

This language of "knitting" souls together in friendship calls to mind Psalm 139, in which the speaker addresses God:

❝You knitted me together in my mother's womb. I praise you, for I am wondrously made. Wonderful are your works!

The Blessed Trinity, who knitted each one of us together in the womb, has also written in our hearts the need for communion. Since, in Christ, we can also recognize the splendor of God shining in another person, we can, in some sense, experience this "knitting together" of souls. There's a union of being which we can't fully articulate, but it seems to whisper to a lost vision which is restored in Jesus Christ.

A final example is Philippians 1:7–8. St. Paul writes to the Christians in Philippi:

❝It is right for me to feel this way, about you all, because I hold you in my heart … For God is my witness, how I long for you all with the affection of Christ Jesus.

St. Paul is not speaking facetiously—in fact the Greek word we translate as "affection" actually means my inmost self, my deep heart's core. Jesus has given St. Paul a glimpse of his own vision of each person, and what occurs in Paul's heart naturally spills over into his words and his actions.

This recognition, which becomes union of being with the one recognized, is given back to us in the Paschal Mystery. Therefore it's inseparable from our own participation in Christ's Passion, Death, and Resurrection, which we entered in our baptism and live out in the daily realities of our lives. We have been redeemed; all things have been made new. In the midst of our own glaring brokenness (and the glaring brokenness of others) we can participate in a new vision through which, in Christ, all things are united. Communion is not an empty dream or an abstract project, it is a gift.

Is there any promise more wonderful than that? Is there any calling more moving (and more committing) than that? This recognition takes root as an attitude in our hearts, and this attitude is what we'll explore in the following section.

QUESTIONS FOR FURTHER REFLECTION

1. Do I truly allow myself to be recognized by God—as I am? What is my greatest fear or struggle in this regard?

2. How would I describe my experience of receiving Christ in the Eucharist?

3. Why do I agree (or disagree) with the possibility of union of being with others? In what aspects?

4. In what ways have I had a taste of this union of being with another person? What does that tell me about God? About others? About myself?

ATTITUDE

❝ If we allow Christ to touch our heart we will begin to experience God's love as a transforming power that cures and restores … It is the experience of a new, gratuitous, unlimited, and unconditional love, which fills our soul with joy and security.

—*Regnum Christi Member Handbook*, number 29

❝ All these are hints and guesses, hints followed by guesses … The hint half guessed, the gift half understood, is Incarnation.

—T.S. Eliot, "The Dry Salvages"

A GIFT DULY NOTED

In *Leisure, the Basis of Culture*, Joseph Pieper observes: "Man seems to mistrust everything that is effortless; he can only enjoy what he has acquired with toil and trouble; he refuses to have anything as a gift." Do we sometimes treat interpersonal communion in a similar manner—as a task to be accomplished than as a gift to be received?

This is not to say that it is effortless. To be open and receptive requires effort. Communion certainly requires effort. And yet it's much more the effort of Mary's "Let it be done to me according to your word," than of Peter's "Lord, though everyone should deny you I will never deny you." Interpersonal communion requires a recognition that acknowledges the gift that the other is for me.

In this vision we begin to discover that every person is a gift. Saint John Paul II describes it beautifully:

When man discovers the disinterested gift that the other human person is to him, it is as if he discovers the whole world in that other person.

The Polish writer Henryk Sienkiewicz seems to intuit this truth, giving it eloquent expression towards the end of his novel *Quo Vadis*. The Christian patrician Marcus Vinicius is in the garden of his villa gazing upon the face of his sleeping fiancé, Lygia, who was nearly executed by Emperor Nero. As she slowly recovers her health after the ordeal, lines of sorrow and suffering are still etched deeply into her face. Yet suddenly it occurred to Vinicius that "as he stood watching over her, he was watching over the whole world." The world in which we live is similarly suffering and yet redeemed.

This communion, or union of being with the one recognized, is an attitude that God wants to give us. We experience it in a personal way—with our own temperament, history, interests, strengths and weaknesses—but there are some common characteristics.

SOME CHARACTERISTICS

First, we experience communion as a growing awareness of the other person as another person. The author Eckhart Tolle describes how this realization helped bring him back from the brink of suicide. He was struck by wonder at the presence of another person, of all people. For months he spent hours each day simply marveling at the people who walked by. That experience is a window into the heart of God, who created us as free beings and yet who longs to become one with us.

And secondly, we need to realize that this awareness—which is really a new vision—shapes our hearts. Since we are persons, this means that it gradually shapes our whole being, including our feelings. This isn't the result of simply deciding that our lives would be easier if we possessed such a vision, and then mapping a game plan to obtain it. It's not a workout program. It's the mysterious and deeply felt relationship between our freedom and God's grace; it's the gift freely given which we freely receive; it's God's gift that we give back as ourselves.

I can recall a moment of deep interpersonal tension (translation: I was furious with someone and couldn't stand to be around him), and I was discussing this with my spiritual director. He listened and then queried "Have you asked God to show you how that person is a gift to you?" I admitted that nothing could be farther from my mind, but decided to give it a try. And after several weeks of this something shifted. I still felt that I didn't really click with him, but at deeper level there was a growing sense of communion which changed our interaction. There were still squabbles and frustrations—sinfulness doesn't just evaporate—but there was a sense of recognition and respect, stemming not from what he (and I) could or couldn't do, but from his simply being another human person and a member of the same spiritual family. That is everything, and that is enough.

This new vision is one into which we slowly grow. We still make mistakes and suffer occasional, or even frequent, misunderstandings. But we can ask God to shape our hearts, to give us this gift of communion, born of an attitude flowing from a heart made new in the Paschal Mystery. Communion is Baptism integrated and integrating; it is the relational core of all we are and all we do.

ACTIVE RELATIONSHIP

With all that in mind, I'd like to loop back to the initial thesis: communion as union of being with the one recognized is above all an attitude of the heart, a new vision received as a gift. What, exactly, is an attitude? In his *Sources of Renewal*, Saint John Paul II put it like this:

> An attitude is an active relationship that is not yet action, but that disposes us towards action.

This is moving towards communion as mission, and yet its foundation is an understanding similar to Pope Benedict's assertion that communion is a union of being with the one recognized, a communion which is expressed in a new relationship.

In the Symposium Plato maintained that the purpose of worship is to heal our love, and this is above all a plea for redeemed relationships. Ezekiel 36:26 sheds more light on this desire.

❝A new heart I will give you, and a new spirit I will put within you, and you will be clean from all your uncleanness, and from all your idols I will cleanse you.

But what sort of heart will this be, and how will we know its authenticity? I Peter 1:22 provides a clue.

❝Having purified your souls by your obedience to the truth for a sincere love of the brethren, love one another earnestly from the heart.

Living in communion with Christ, which requires obedience to the truth, translates into loving one another earnestly from the heart. This is the new heart that Ezekiel prophesied, a heart that makes possible and safeguards the redeemed relationships for which Plato longed. The heart is the core of who I am—body, mind, will, emotions, and affections. The heart is where I choose, where I receive love and give love.

The gift of a new heart helps explain Saint John Paul II's description of attitude. Because Christ has made all things new, the baptized Christian lives in a new relationship with all of creation. But this gift applies first and foremost to our relationships with our fellow human beings, who like us are created to love and be loved. Our relationship with them begins in the heart before it takes the form of action. Our new vision is redemptive because it born of a heart redeemed by Christ.

Here it might be helpful to pause for a moment and consider the etymology of "relationship." The word contains a deep truth about what it means to be human, created in the image and likeness of God, who is a communion of persons. Relationship comes from the Latin word *relatus*, which is the past participle of *referre*: to bring back, to carry back, to restore—a striking etymology. In our redemption, Christ has restored to us the embrace of Trinitarian love. At the same time, our redeemed relationships with others play an essential part in completing and expressing that restoration. We are redeemed: Christ has brought us back to the Father. Yet we work out our salvation in communion with others, in those redeemed relationships that continually restore us.

Communion then is a recognition, a union of being, an active relationship that's not yet action but is moving us towards action. That action, or mission, is what we'll explore in the next section.

Let's set the stage for the next point by linking communion and mission through the lovely language of poetry. The Jesuit poet Gerard Manley Hopkins captured the essence of communion in his poem "As Kingfishers Catch Fire." The second stanza touches upon the deep mystery of the Word made Flesh and our belonging to that mystery.

... I say more: the just man justices;
Keeps grace: that keeps all his goings graces;
Acts in God's eye what in God's eye he is—
Christ—or Christ plays in ten thousand places,
Lovely in limbs, and lovely in eyes not his
To the Father through the features of men's faces.

QUESTIONS FOR FURTHER REFLECTION

1. How do I experience God's vision of me?

2. How does God know me? How do I know God? What role does my heart play in all this?

3. How do I glory in the gift of being human? If this is difficult for me, why?

COMMUNION AND MISSION

❝ Our mission crystallizes when each one of our members makes God's love known to others in any life situation whatsoever, and in any sector of society. Therefore, whenever a member of Regnum Christi lives and preaches love, there the mission of Regnum Christi is being carried out.

—*Regnum Christi Member Handbook*, Number 42

❝ Let every one of you become a chorus of song, so that in the harmony of your concord, adopting the melody of God in unity, you will sing for the Father with one voice in Christ Jesus.

—Ignatius of Antioch, *Letter to the Ephesians*

Where does Regnum Christi fit in with everything said so far? We're deeply aware of the missionary dimension our Baptism imparts, and the corresponding call to evangelize. The full beauty of our charism invites us to explore further our call to mission and evangelization.

Recognition begs for expression. What's our first reaction when struck by the beauty and wonder of a sunset, or a waterfall, or the light upon the leaves of trees? We want to share it with someone else. We could almost say "I want to share my recognition—communion—with someone else."

Our desire to share the experience of communion thus becomes mission. This happens naturally and necessarily, without frenetic effort or frenzied efficiency. In John 20:21, on that very beautiful "First Day," the risen Christ tells his disciples:

As the Father has sent me, even so I send you.

The structure is remarkably similar to John 15:9:

As the Father has loved me, so I have loved you; abide in my love. If you keep my commandments, you will abide in my love …

Several lines later, in John 15:12, Jesus reveals what it means to abide in his love:

This is my commandment, that you love one another as I have loved you.

In the Blessed Trinity, communion is at the heart of mission: the Father sends the Son, and the Father and the Son send the Spirit. In fact mission means "the state of being sent" (from the Latin *mittere*); and the Son and the Spirit are sent to draw us back into communion with God. Therefore allowing ourselves to be loved by God is already participation in mission, because it is a participation in the inner life of the Blessed Trinity, in that beauty which is love recognized, received, and poured out.

This is what we share with others. We are sent from love and for love. When we have received the love of God who has sought us and found us in Jesus Christ, we want to propose this love to others. We are filled with joy because we are not alone; we are not forgotten; we are not meaningless.

Mission means revealing communion as the core of existence. We allow ourselves to become mirrors—at once painfully indistinct and luminously clear—in which others can recognize who they already are in the heart of God.

ECHOES OF THE TRINITY

Andrei Rublev's Trinity Icon expresses the unity of communion and mission as only an inspired artist could. It depicts the Blessed Trinity seated around a table, on which a sacred vessel rests. The Father and the Son gaze into each others' eyes, and each is pointing towards the Holy Spirit. There's a wonderful sense of peace and delight in the presence of the Other, which is also fully open to the Third. This sense of invitation does not end with the figure of the Holy Spirit. The outward-pointing staff and the position of his feet poised for motion seem to indicate that this Communion of Persons—perfect and eternal—is extended towards something else, or someone else. Thus the communion within the Blessed Trinity is communicated to creation and in a special way to the human person.

This inner dynamic of communion as mission takes place around the sacred vessel, which holds the Paschal Lamb. Christ restored the gift of communion to us by his

Suffering, Death, and Resurrection. We first received that gift in our baptism; Christ renews it every time we receive his Body and Blood. And by our communion with him, we are fully invested in that same work of redemption. In other words, we share His mission.

COMMUNION OR MISSION?

At times one might assume that communion and mission are, at worst, antithetical and, at best, parallel. This assumption may arise because communion, if understood as a union of being, takes time. Anyone who has tried to live in communion knows that it involves suffering and setbacks and the passage of time. We must make an effort to be open and receptive to the other. We must invest time to reflect on what we receive from the other. Communion requires us to reach out, with thoughtfulness and courage. Add the variables of your own subjective perspective into the mix, and things get gloriously uncontrollable indeed.

Is it worth the effort? Couldn't we just settle for a sort of general détente, in which everyone more or less works together in order to get on with the mission?

This is a false dichotomy, and one that has little appeal on paper. However in the workaday reality in which we live, in the frequent frustrations and in the unintended slights, it's more than a fugitive risk.

We need to recognize that communion is where eternity and time meet. For time and communion are not enemies. Time exists for the sake of communion; it's the unfolding of communion in our lives and in the world. Time is the space God created for communion. There's not too much of it, or too little.

Because what, in the end, are we proposing to the world? Jesus mapped it out in John 17: 21–22 when he prayed:

❝
… That they may all be one; even as you, Father, are in me, and I in you, that they also may be in us, so that the world may believe that you have sent me. The glory which you have given me I have given to them that they may be one even as we are one …

Jesus' words point to a deep union of being, a union of hearts which involves all that we are, a union that unfolds in and through time.

In his *Apologeticum*, the 3rd century Christian writer Tertullian described the pagan world's reaction to the communion that existed among early Christians: "See, they say, *how they love one another*." Those around us are unconsciously longing for a similar experience. If we see love incarnated, if we experience it in our hearts, then there's a hope that we, too, might be given that gift. I remember a homily in which I referred to our inability to truly see our own faces unless they're mirrored in the face of someone who loves us. A young woman asked me afterwards, "But where will I find that? Can someone ever show me that?" In Christ, each one of is a syllable of that question's answer.

Our call to mission means offering communion to others. In *Christifideles Laici*, Saint John Paul II wrote that

❝Communion and mission are profoundly connected with each other, they interpenetrate and mutually imply each other, to the point that communion represents both the source and the fruit of mission: communion gives rise to mission and mission is accomplished in communion.

Mission is sharing the conviction of being recognized, known, and loved as I am. The joy of the Gospel is never encountered in isolation, but in a communion of persons.

Pope Francis echoed this reality in a homily he gave in Quito, Peru:

❝The desire for unity involves the delightful and comforting joy of evangelizing, the conviction that we have an immense treasure to share, one which grows stronger from being shared, and becomes ever more sensitive to the needs of others … We need to entrust our hearts to our companions along the way, without suspicion or distrust …

❝Such unity is already an act of mission, so "that the world may believe" … Evangelization is attracting by our witness those who are far off, in humbly drawing near to those who feel distant from God and the Church, those who are fearful or indifferent, and saying to them: "The Lord, with great respect and love, is also calling you to be a part of his people."

So should we focus on communion or mission? The question answers itself. Communion is mission, as we share the love of God given to us in Jesus Christ.

QUESTIONS FOR FURTHER REFLECTION

1. What is my most memorable experience of sharing Christ with others?

2. In what ways is communion with each other already "mission?"

3. What are some practical ways I can live out communion and mission in my own team, section, and parish?

RECOGNITION, COMMUNION, AND REGNUM CHRISTI

COMMUNION, MISSION, AND DISCERNMENT

Ecclesial movements are generally characterized by a strong missionary dynamism, rooted in the evangelizing vocation of the faithful.

—*Regnum Christi Member Handbook*, Number 10

Spiritually meaningful things never happened in the Church because someone decided to do them, but because God found someone available to welcome him in such a radical way that he could manifest himself and carry out his redemption.

—Marko Rupnik, S.J.,
Discernment, Acquiring the Heart of God

Is there a practical key to communion as mission? On an operative level, what provides the reassurance that mission truly flows from communion and leads back to it? What guarantees that this union of being with the one recognized is actually expressed as mission?

Without delving too deeply into the subject of discernment here are several principles that help us to live in communion as mission, and vice versa.

HOW DOES GOD COMMUNICATE WITH US?

In a world of instant results, it's easy to form the idea that we decide, and something happens. I decide to invest in a certain stock option, and my bank account grows. I decide to get a membership at a gym, and I get back in shape (or I would, except for those demonic blueberry muffins that mysteriously find their way onto my plate). The pattern we expect is this: my decision leads to effort, and my effort leads to a result.

But this pattern does not apply to our relationship with God. Of course we have a choice to make, but that choice is whether to *accept* what God offers us in Jesus Christ. The initiative is God's, and it flows from Trinitarian communion, from a passionate Love that wants to share itself.

The revelation of God as a communion of persons—as love—attains perfect expression in the Incarnation. God does not communicate an idea or a concept; he communicates himself in a dialogue of love that fills Sacred Scripture from the first lines of Genesis. Actually, we could say that communication is the act of communing, the process by which communion is offered to the other. Jesus Christ is the fullness of revelation, of God's communication of himself to us. In Jesus, God speaks himself and gives himself to us. As St. Irenaeus of Lyon forcefully pointed out, "God made himself the very thing we are, to make of us that which he is."

All of this means that God really does communicate with us in a number of ways. He does so through Sacred Scripture and Sacred Tradition, which, interpreted by the Holy Father and the bishops in communion with him, form the one source of revelation. He communicates with us through the events of our lives, and through our thoughts and feelings. Therefore it follows that God respects our humanity. He created it. And in the Incarnation he bound himself to us with a bond that can never be broken. Therefore God communicates himself to us in a form adapted to our humanity and in a manner which exalts the goodness and the gift of being human. Living in a union of being with the one recognized—with the Blessed Trinity and therefore with others—means a growing sense of what that communion requires, and an increasing awareness of what nourishes it and what wounds it. And when love is lessened, the heart refuses to be silent.

AWARENESS, UNDERSTANDING, ACTION

In his various books on discernment, Fr. Timothy Gallagher returns again and again to a core concept: discernment means awareness, understanding, and action. Since communion as mission clearly implies action, let's take a brief look at what he means.

○   Awareness. I can be increasingly aware of which thoughts and feelings are most prevalent in my heart. What are they? What reaction does this or that particular event cause?

- o Understanding. As we become more aware of our interior world, we can begin to understand those movements of the heart. Where does that thought or that feeling come from? Is it in keeping with my identity as a beloved son or daughter of God? If I were to follow it, where would it lead? Would it bring me to recognize the other, or would it carry me towards isolation and cause me to close in on myself? Would it bring a subtle harm to others?

- o Action. After praying about this (and hopefully discussing it with a spiritual director), I'll act. This thought or this feeling, and the inspiration to act that flows from them, should be accepted or rejected.

Clearly not every inspiration comes from God. And even inspirations that seem good, that seem to imply mission, may not come from God. For example, if this project or possibility, good in and of itself, wounds or bypasses communion (in the Body of Christ in general, or in the part of that Body to which God has called me), we should pause for thought and further prayer.

That brings up another important point. We do not discern in isolation, because we do not exist in isolation. Isolation is, quite literally, hell (the absence of communion).

J.R.R. Tolkien graphically depicted this when he described Melkor's fall in the *Silmarillion* (Melkor represents Lucifer in Tolkien's mythology).

To Melkor had been given the greatest gifts of power and knowledge, and he had a share in all the gifts of his brethren. He had gone often alone into the Void seeking the Imperishable Flame … Yet he found not the Fire … But being alone he had begun to conceive thoughts of his own unlike those of his brethren.

He was searching for something good (actually, in Tolkien's cosmology this "Imperishable Flame" represents the Holy Spirit), but he looked for it in isolation. And anyone who has read the *Silmarillion* knows how Melkor ended up, and the havoc he wreaked upon the world.

True mission must be discerned in communion, not in isolation (hence the spiritual masters' insistence on spiritual direction). If a particular inspiration or opportunity affects those closest to me, then they should be involved in the discernment. The level of their involvement depends on the level of importance the decision has.

The task of discernment requires a tremendous respect for the other, and great confidence in those at my side. Returning to the quote from Pope Francis in an earlier section, shared discernment means that "We need to entrust our hearts to our companions along the way, without suspicion or distrust …"

NOT AFRAID

From this place of peace, a beautiful mission is born. From recognition, a communion of hearts comes into being. There is an awareness that I need the other, not to merely fulfill a mission but simply to be. And by the infinite mercy of God, I, too, am necessary for the other; I, too, reveal the face of God.

This experience brings to life the stirring statement attributed to St. Ignatius Loyola:

❝Not to be daunted by the greatest undertaking, yet to also invest oneself even in the smallest, this is divine.

The word "invest", though brief, carries considerable significance. It recalls Christ's words to the disciples at the miracle of the multiplication of the loaves:

❝Give them something yourselves.

—Mark 6

It also echoes the exclamation that burst from the heart of Jesus when he saw the poor widow place her two copper coins into the temple treasury:

❝Truly I tell you, this poor widow has put in more than all of them … she, out of her poverty, put in all that she had.

—Luke 21:3–4

In the same way, St. Ignatius had deeply felt Christ's words, "Without cost you have received, without cost you are to give." (Matthew 10:8). What have we received as a gift? Jesus. In Christ, we receive ourselves. Therefore, we can truly invest in the well-being of others; we can be fully present to others because God is fully present to us.

Whether the undertaking seems great or small is irrelevant; all God asks is that we be present in it. It doesn't matter if it's an apostolate with international implications, or simply taking the time to reach out to someone who's suffering and alone. All God asks is that we be present in that gift.

In 2 Timothy 12, St. Paul proclaims:

❝ I know him in whom I have put my trust.

And that growing trust in God slowly shapes the way we see those God has given to us. We recognize them as sons and daughters of God, wounded and flawed like all of us, and still worthy of our trust. This does not mean a naïvely feckless attitude; it implies that we trust in Christ's power to make all things new, and that we offer that conviction to those God has put at our side.

Pope Francis summed this up at the end of his previously cited homily, when he said:

❝ Giving of ourselves establishes an interpersonal relationship; we do not give "things" but our very selves. In any act of giving, we give ourselves. "Giving of oneself" means letting all the power of that love which is the Spirit of God take root in our lives ... When we give of ourselves, we discover our true identity as children of God in the image of the Father and, like him, givers of life; we discover that we are brothers and sisters of Jesus, to whom we bear witness. This is what it means to evangelize; this is our revolution—because our faith is always revolutionary, this is our deepest and most enduring cry.

As we give ourselves, we better understand the aforementioned Ignatian maxim, which seems so relevant for Regnum Christi: "Not to be daunted by the greatest undertaking, yet to also invest oneself fully in even the smallest, this is divine." And by Christ's Incarnation such investment, precisely because it's divine, is also wonderfully human.

QUESTIONS FOR FURTHER REFLECTION

Here are a few core questions to ask ourselves when discerning any inspiration to mission.

1. How is our Lord involved in this decision-making process?

2. What is our core identity-as-gift (charism), and does this opportunity match that? Can we articulate how?

3. What is my individual identity-as-gift (personal charism), and does this opportunity match that? Can I articulate how?

4. If communion is the person recognized and expressed (a union of being with the one recognized), how does this opportunity express that?

5. What does it mean that mission flows from communion and leads back to it? How does this particular opportunity uphold that, or would it wound communion?

EPILOGUE

What you long for will be given you; what you love will be yours forever.

—St. Leo the Great, Sermon 95

*There we will rest and we will see; we will see and we will love, we will love and we will praise. Such will be the end, without end.

—St. Augustine, *City of God*

Thomas Merton's experience of communion recounted at the beginning of this reflection was not an illusion or a quixotic dream. We have all experienced something similar at different moments in our lives—most vividly, perhaps, within Regnum Christi. In my own case, the experience of communion and its relationship to mission has made all the difference.

In the midst of the tremendous turmoil of 2009 and the ensuing years, I often asked myself: "None of this seems to make any sense … Does God want me here?" But when I looked around at the individual Regnum Christi members I knew—Legionaries, consecrated men and women, families—I realized that God was speaking to me through them: he was making himself present through them. The God who became man is still, it seems, incarnational. The God who is interpersonal communion creates that same communion as his greatest gift.

This was a truth that surpassed rules or regulations; it eclipsed what Chesterton called those "tangled things, texts and aching eyes"; it was an undeniable personal presence that brought hope and peace. Many problems in our lives begin when we lose ourselves in abstraction, and forget the person in front of us or at our side.

Christ invites us to recognize that communion is given as a gift; and accepting the gift also means giving it back. Communion is not my own heroic endeavor, in which

I define the rules of engagement and the operational timeline. Communion requires asking for, and becoming increasingly open to, the union of being with the one recognized that God himself wills and creates.

Communion, to return to the initial thesis, is an attitude of the heart, which is recognition of the other and a reverence that flows over into our thoughts, our words, and our actions. It's the result of something God has already done, in the Paschal Mystery of his Passion, Death and Resurrection. The gift is communicated to us in the sacrament of Baptism, restored in the Sacrament of Reconciliation, and constantly made new in the great Sacrament of Christ's love, the Eucharist. Awareness of this is life.

Here Mary comes to mind:

> She kept all these things in her heart.
>
> —Luke 2:51

In Greek, the word we translate as "kept"—*sunterei*—has a particular nuance of "keeping safe." In Jesus we are forever safe in the heart of God:

> You are precious in my eyes, and glorious, and I love you.
>
> —Isaiah 43:7

And Mary, filled with the Holy Spirit, images this: she keeps us safe in her heart and shows us that we have the same mission. In those redeemed relationships that flow from communion and lead back to it, we are kept safe and we participate in that "keeping safe" of the other.

As we allow this vision of communion to pervade our hearts, action becomes a necessity; and it will be an action that is truly communion as mission and mission as communion. Ours is to ask for that communion flowing from a heart made new, to offer to God the frustration of our sinfulness that so often impedes it, and to trust, with a confidence storm-tossed but always undismayed, that in Christ we can offer this to every person we meet.

Please visit our website, *RCSpirituality.org* for more spiritual resources, and follow us on Facebook for regular updates: *facebook.com/RCSpirituality*

Regnum Christi Essays are a service of Regnum Christi and the Legionaries of Christ.
RegnumChristi.org & LegionofChrist.org

Produced by Coronation.
CoronationMedia.com

Developed & Self-published by RCSpirituality.
RCSpirituality.org

Made in the USA
Middletown, DE
23 October 2020